Published by: Kansas City Star Books
1729 Grand Blvd.
Kansas City, Missouri, USA 64108

First edition, first printing
ISBN: 978-1-935362-85-2

Library of Congress Control Number:
2009924512

Printed in the United States of America by Walsworth Publishing Co., Marceline, Missouri

To order copies, call toll-free 866-834-7467.

The Quilter's Home Page

www.PickleDish.com
www.PickleDishStore.com

My Stars V

Patterns from The Kansas City Star • Volume V

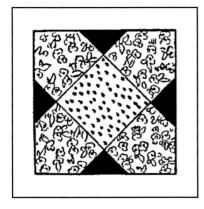
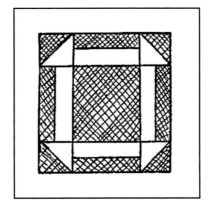

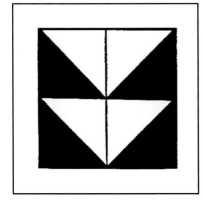
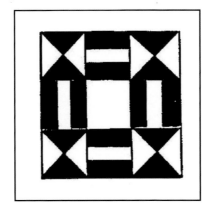
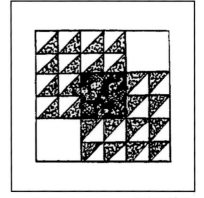

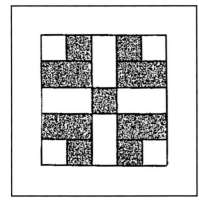
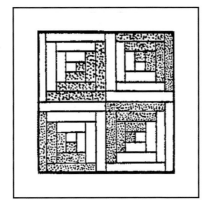

INTRODUCTION

We've crossed the 100-pattern mark, and are now onto patterns 100 to 125! This crop of patterns has some of my favorites – The Pig Pen, Molly's Rose Garden, and Rob Peter and Pay Paul, to name a few. It also includes classics such as Log Cabin, Victory Quilt, and A Fan of Many Colors. All 25 patterns in this volume are charming and provide endless opportunities for quiltmaking.

Be sure to check out the photographs of the gorgeous quilts that accompany some of the blocks. The quilt contributors had lots of fun making new quilts with these historical patterns. It's always exciting to see a new twist!

The Kansas City Star began printing traditional quilt patterns in 1928. The patterns were a weekly feature in The Star or its sister publications, The Weekly Star and The Star Farmer, from 1928 until the mid-1930s, then less regularly until 1961. By the time the last one ran, more than 1,000 had been published in the papers, which circulated in seven Midwestern states as well as North Carolina, Kentucky and Texas.

The *My Stars* series is Kansas City Star Quilts' effort to redraft the entire historical collection, and offer it in bound printed volumes for pattern lovers to stitch and collect. Each of the 25 patterns in this book includes fabric requirements, templates and assembly instructions, as well as the original sketch and caption that were printed in the newspaper. Sit back and enjoy the heritage of quilting with this fifth installment.

-Diane McLendon, editor

*   *   *

ACKNOWLEDGEMENTS

I would like to thank the wonderful team that has made My Star Collection and the *My Stars* series possible: Edie McGinnis, Jenifer Dick, Kim Walsh, Jane Miller, Doug Weaver, Aaron Leimkuehler, Jo Ann Groves, and of course, our quilt friends who have graciously provided their quilts to be included in this book.

-Diane McLendon, editor

*   *   *

My Star Collection is a weekly subscription service where subscribers download a pdf pattern – from The Kansas City Star's historical 1928 to 1961 collection – each week. The subscription is for a year of patterns – 52 in all. For more information or to sign up, visit subscriptions.pickledish.com.

TABLE OF CONTENTS

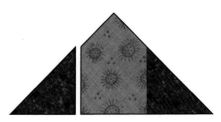

Mountain Peak

Block Size: 12" finished

Fabric Needed

Dark blue

Medium blue

Light blue

Since this block has some odd shapes, we will be using templates.

Cutting Instructions

From the dark blue fabric, cut

4 triangles using template B or 1 – 7 3/16" square. Cut the square from corner to corner twice on the diagonal.

From the light blue fabric, cut

1 – 4 3/4" square or use template C

From the medium blue fabric, cut

4 pieces using template A

To Make the Block

1 Sew a dark blue triangle to either side of a medium blue A piece. Make two rows like this.

2 Sew a medium blue A piece to either side of the light blue C square. Make one row.

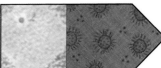

3 Sew a medium blue A piece to either side of the light blue C square. Make one row.

Mountain Peak

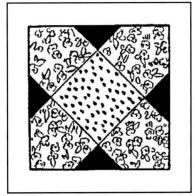

From The Kansas City Star,

July 7, 1943:

No. 722

Original size – 9 1/2"

Caption: Light colored prints against a dark background establish the purpose of this design offered by Mrs. S. B. Brown, Route 1, Collins, Ark.

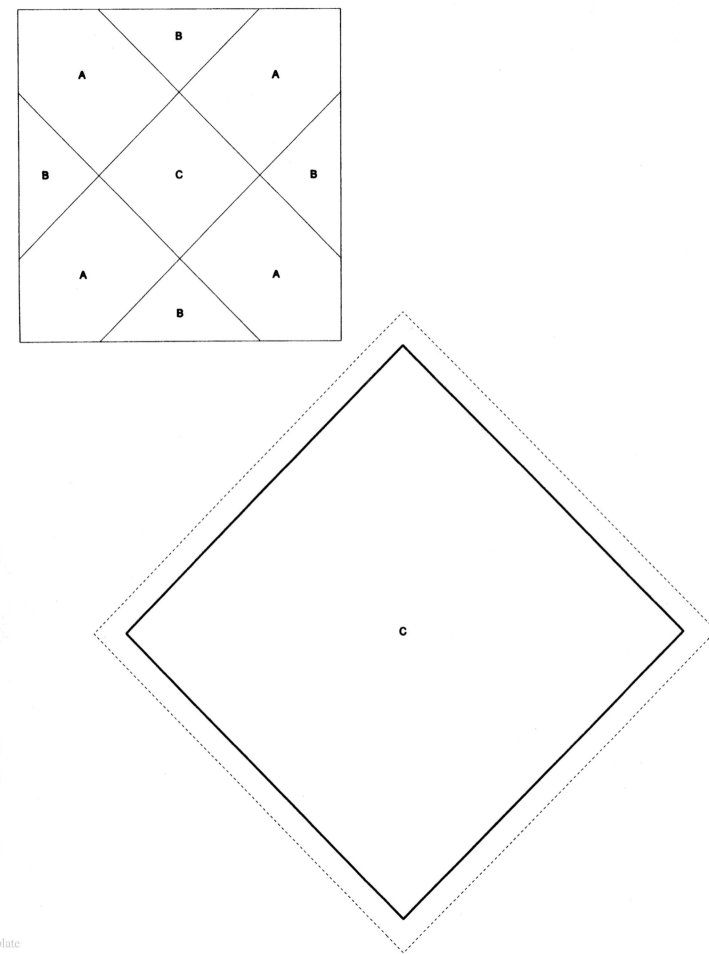

Mountain Peak

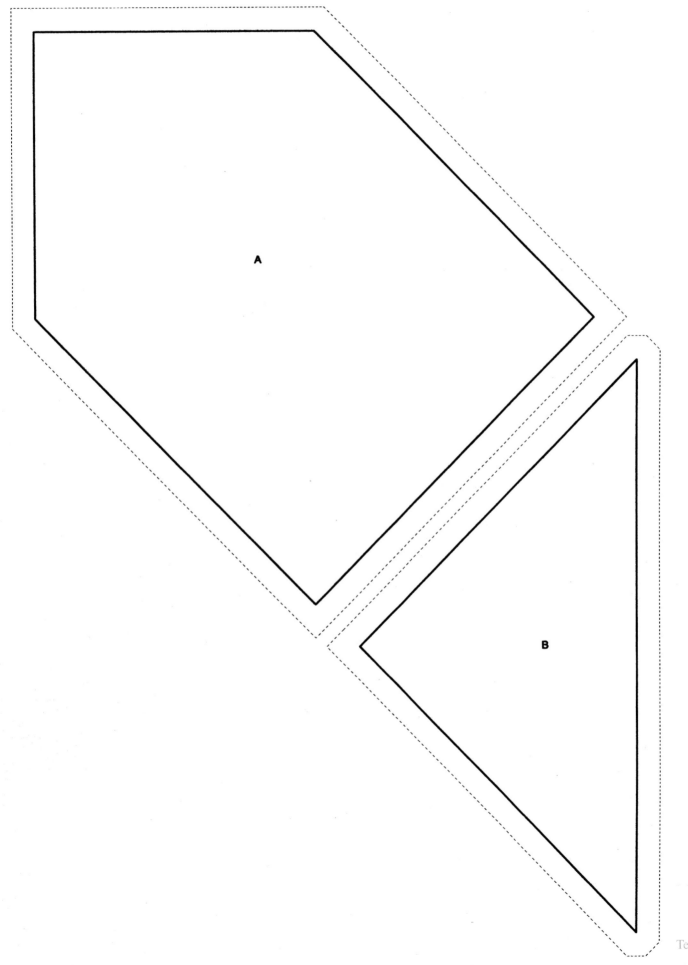

A

B

Mountain Peak

Template

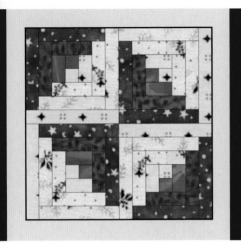

Log Cabin

Block Size: 12" finished

Fabric Needed

Three reds

Four lights

(We used shirtings in

the example.)

This week is a paper piecing pattern. Please note there are two sections – A and B. The only difference is the way they are turned.

Cutting Directions

Cut 1 1/2" wide strips from each of your fabrics.

They will be of differing lengths and should be at least 1/2" longer than necessary.

To Make the Block

1

Copy 2 each Copy 2 each of Section A and Section B.

Paper piece 2 of Section A and 2 of section B. Follow the diagram for color placement.

After all the fabric is sewn to the paper, trim the outside along the dotted line. That will give you 1/4" seam allowance. Sew the four sections together as shown to complete the block.

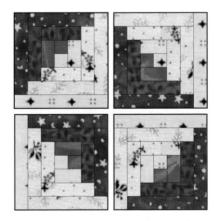

Log Cabin

Section A   Section B

Section B   Section A

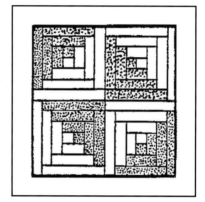

Original size – 13 3/4"
This pattern, one originating with the early American pioneers, should appeal to the lovers of cross-word puzzles, as well as quilt fans, for it must be watched constantly to avoid mistakes. There are numerous arrangements of this block, as can be seen by changing the positions of the four sections. If figured materials are used, be sure to use the light and dark ones for contrast, otherwise use plain colors. This makes a very handsome all-over design for quilt or coverlet, and can be made of many small scraps of silk or cotton or linen.

History of the Block

Connecticut Colors designed and quilted by Patricia Hersl, Milton, DE.

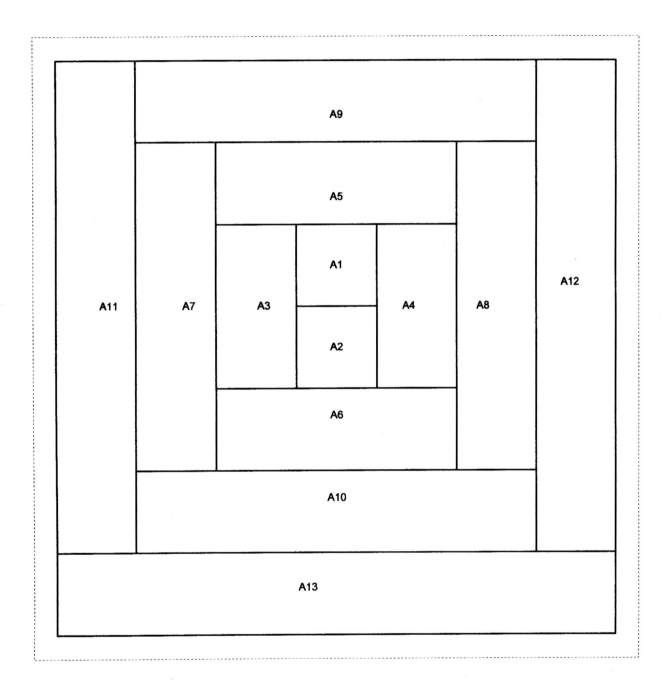

Log Cabin

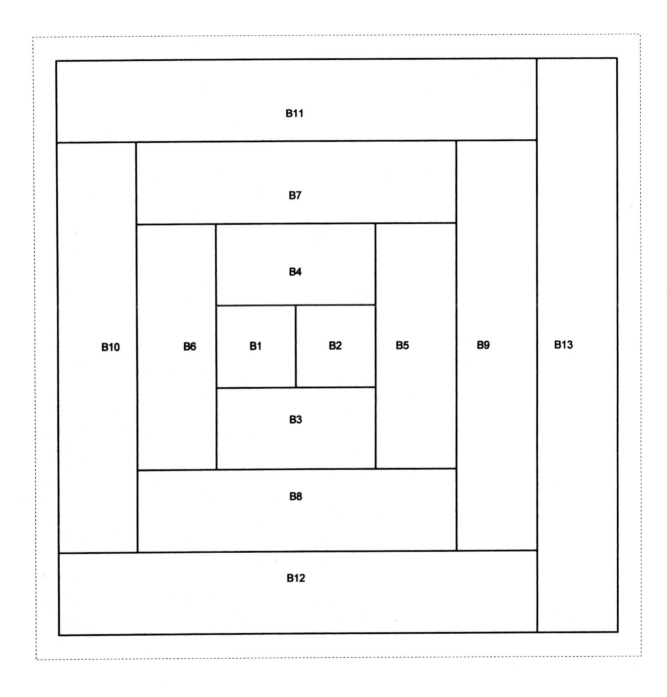

Log Cabin

Template

Picture Frame

Block Size: 12" finished

Fabric Needed

Light orange

Medium orange

Black

Halloween print

To Make the Block

1 Make 4 half-square triangle units. Draw a line from corner to corner on the reverse side of the 2 7/8" light orange squares. Place the light orange squares atop the medium orange squares with right sides facing. Sew 1/4" on either side of the line. Using your rotary cutter, cut along the drawn line. Open the units and press toward the darker fabric.

Sew the light orange strips to the black strips. Make four.

2 Sew a half-square triangle unit to either end of two of the orange/black strips.

3 Sew an orange/black strip unit to either side of the 8 1/2" print square.

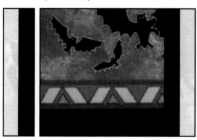

This block would be great for a Halloween quilt. We have provided templates for everything but the center square which is 8". Templates are not needed for this block.

Cutting Directions

From the light orange, cut

4 – 1 1/2" x 8 1/2" strips

2 – 2 7/8" squares

From the medium orange, cut

2 – 2 7/8" squares

From the black, cut

4 – 1 1/2" x 8 1/2" strips

From the Halloween print, cut

1 – 8 1/2" square

Picture Frame

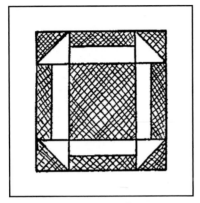

From The Kansas City Star,

September 28, 1955:

No. 963

9" block - pieced.

Thinking of quilt makers who admire older designs, Mrs. Laura Raleigh, Bixby Star route, Salem, Mo., offers this one which is named the Picture Frame.

4

Sew the three rows together to complete the block.

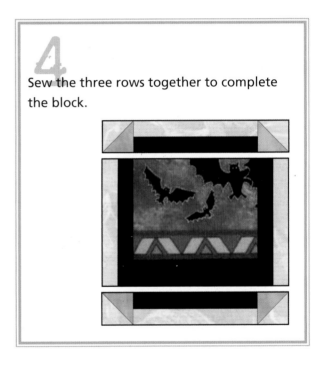

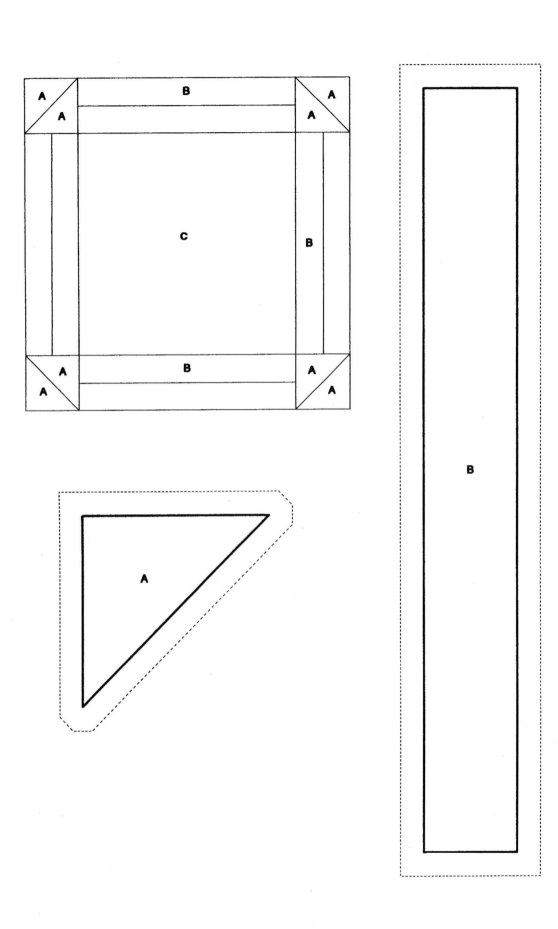

Picture Frame

The Pig Pen

Block Size: 12" finished

Fabric Needed
Brown
Cream shirting

You'll need to use templates for these curved pieces. This block can be completely pieced or partially appliquéd. You'll find both methods below so decide on how you want to make this before you do any cutting.

Cutting Instructions for Piecing the block
From the brown fabric, cut

2 pieces using template A
2 pieces using template B
2 pieces using template C

From the cream shirting, cut

2 pieces using template A
2 pieces using template B
2 pieces using template C

Cutting Instructions for combining appliqué and piecing
From the brown fabric, cut

2 – 6 1/2" squares
2 arcs using template B

From the cream shirting, cut

2 – 6 1/2" squares
2 arcs using template B

To Make the Block

1. If you are piecing the block, sew a cream piece A to a brown piece B. Then add a cream piece C. Make two like this. Then reverse the color scheme and sew a brown piece A to a cream piece B. Add a brown piece C. Make two.

2. Sew the four quadrants together to complete the block.

If you want to use appliqué, press the curved edges of the arcs under and stitch the brown arcs to the cream squares. Then stitch the cream arcs to the brown squares.

The Pig Pen

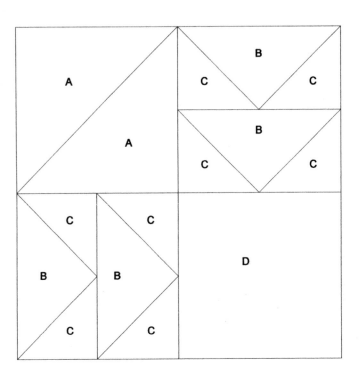

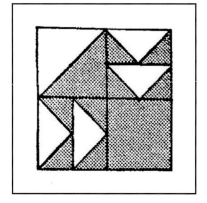

From The Kansas City Star,

February 1, 1939:

No. 569

Original size – 9 1/2"

The "T" quilt block is simple enough in composition, but its chief attraction is in carefully matching all the corners.

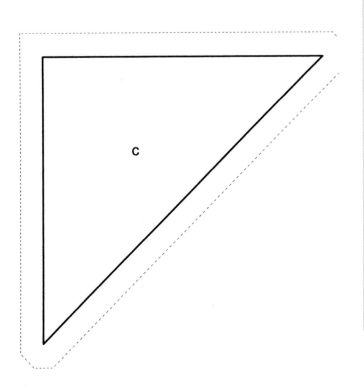

T in Kimonas by Sunisa Cote, Sammamish, WA.
Quilted by Deborah K. Burnett, Simpsonville, SC.

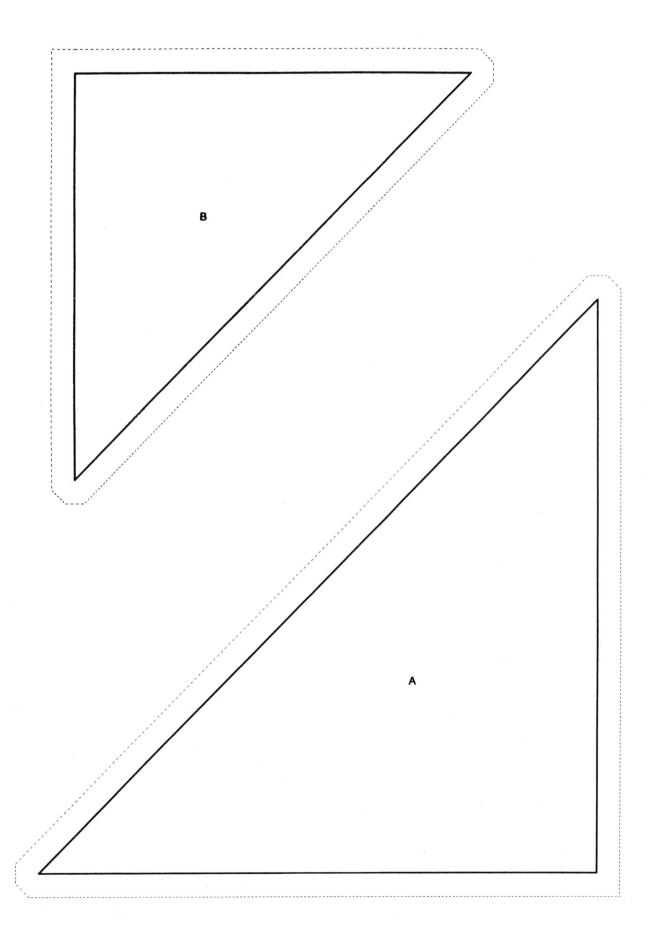

B

A

"T" Quilt

Template

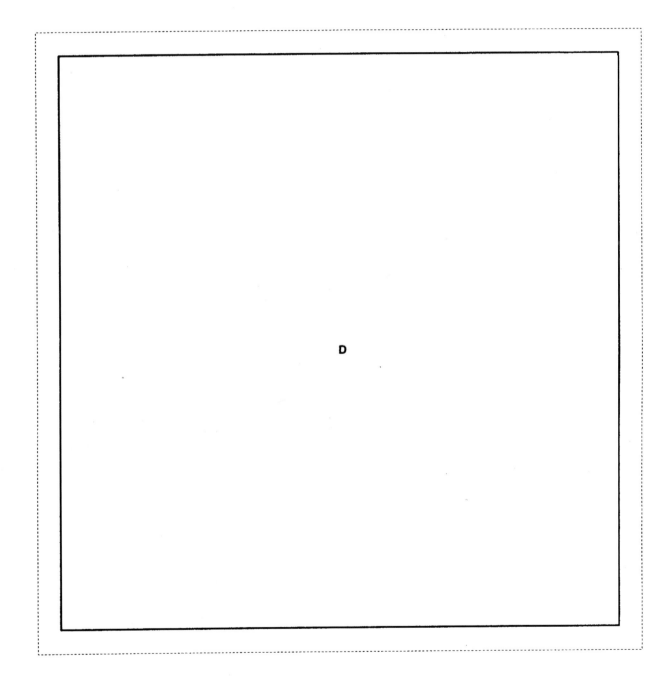

D

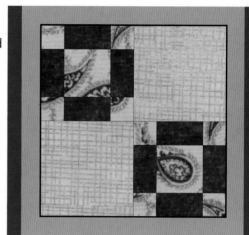

Appeared in The Star **January 31, 1931**

To Make the Block

1 Sew a 2 1/2" square to either end of a dark green rectangle. Make four.

2 Now sew a dark green rectangle to either side of the green print square. Make two.

3 Sew the strips together as shown. Make two. Each of these finished squares makes up one quadrant of the block.

4 Sew the block together as shown.

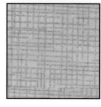

Sheep Fold Quilt

Block Size: 16" finished

Fabric Needed

Dark green

Green print

Tan

The original pattern suggests you gather "the ninety and nine" fabrics and make a scrappy quilt. This could be a great way to use up some of your fabric.

Although we are providing templates for all pieces except the 8 1/2" setting square, everything can be cut using the rotary cutter and ruler.

Cutting Instructions

From the dark green, cut

8 – 4 1/2" x 2 1/2" rectangles

From the green and tan print, cut

8 – 2 1/2" squares

2 – 4 1/2" squares

From the tan fabric, cut

2 – 8 1/2" squares

Sheep Fold Quilt

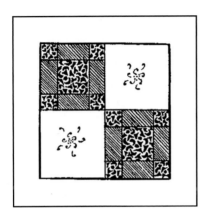

From The Kansas City Star,

Janury 31, 1931:

No. 155

Original 16" block.

For the woman who neither has the time nor the inclination to make intricate quilt designs, "The Sheep Fold Quilt," a very simple pattern, is presented today. Gathering the ninety and nine for the "fold" in this case will be fun. Choose pretty colors and alternate squares of plain and figured fabric for a different effect. The sketch shows two 8-inch squares. Another pleasing development would be to use a pretty floral fabric for the center square and one with dots or circles for the four small squares. Allow for seams.

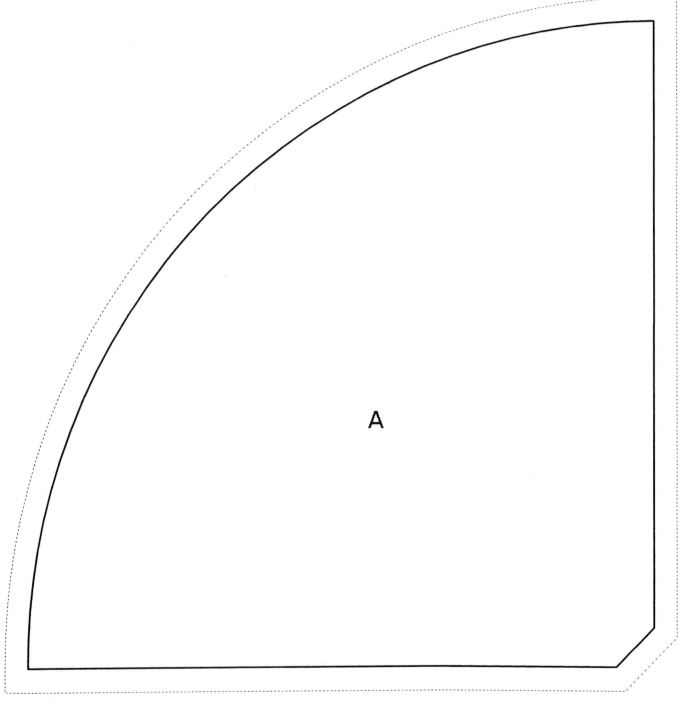

A

Sea Shell

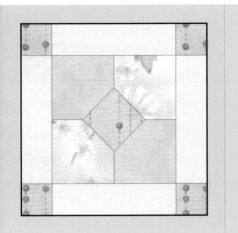

Yellow Square

Block Size: 12" finished

Fabric Needed

Yellow

Yellow print

Pale blue

Blue and yellow print

Because of the odd shape of some of the pieces, we will be using templates.

Cutting Directions

From the yellow print fabric, cut

4 – 2 1/2" squares (template A)

1 – 3 5/16" square (template D)

From the yellow fabric, cut

2 pieces using template C

From the blue and yellow print, cut

2 pieces using template C

From the pale blue fabric, cut

4 – 2 1/2" x 8 1/2" rectangles (template B)

To Make the Block

1

Sew a yellow A square to each end of a pale blue rectangle as shown. Make two.

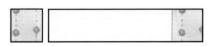

2

Sew the two blue and yellow print C pieces to the D square.

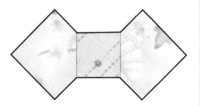

3

Sew the yellow C pieces to the D square, then close the seams between the yellow pieces and the blue/yellow print pieces.
You now have a center square.

4

Sew a pale blue rectangle to either side of the square.

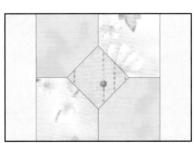

Yellow Square

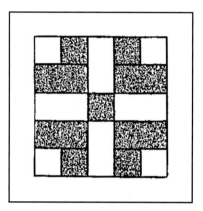

From The Kansas City Star,

July 24, 1940:

No. 621

Original size - 11 1/4"

Miss Jane Bookout, Branson, Mo., has named this the "Double V" pattern. The contributor of the pattern thinks the quilts she has completed of 1-tone blocks are more attractive than those made of prints.

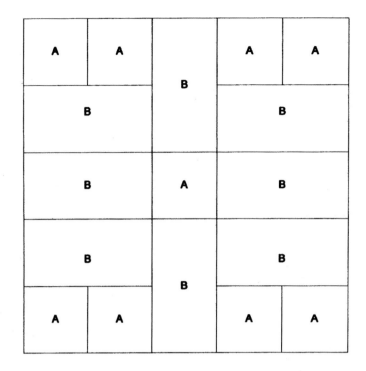

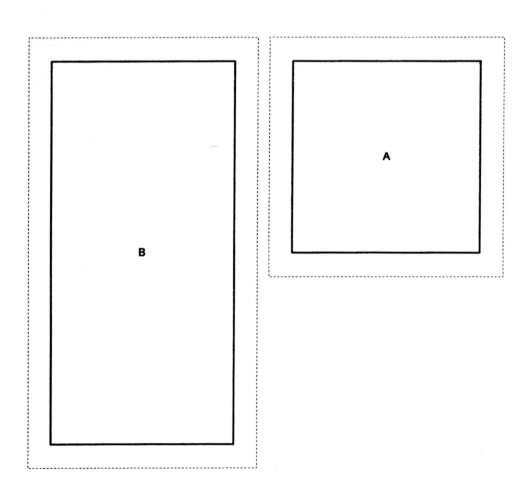

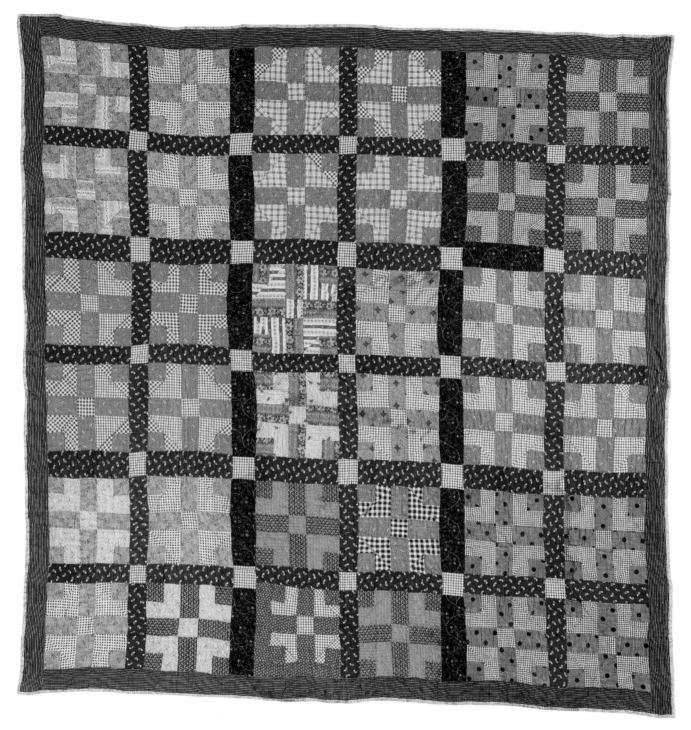

Double V owned by Connie Ryle Neumann, Longmont, CO.
Designer and quilter unknown.

Molly's Rose Garden

Block Size: 9" finished

Fabric Needed

Medium peach

Dark peach

Green

Cream

This block is pieced then appliquéd in place on a background square.

Cutting Instructions

From the green fabric, cut

4 leaves using template B

From the medium peach fabric, cut

4 petals using template A

From the dark peach fabric, cut

1 circle using template C

From the cream fabric, cut

1 – 10" square

Trim the square to 9 1/2" leaving a 1/4" seam allowance on all four sides after the appliqué work is finished.

To Make the Block

1 Fold the cream background square in quarters from corner to corner and lightly press. These creases will help you with the placement of the appliqué pieces.

Sew the 4 petals together. Press the seam allowances on the edges of the flower under. Pin the flower in place by lining up the seam allowances with the creases that go toward the corners.

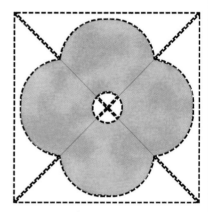

2 Press the seam allowances under on the outer edges of each of the leaves and pin in place. The center and point of each leaf should line up with the crease that goes toward each corner. Tuck the widest end of each leaf under the flower. Appliqué all in place.

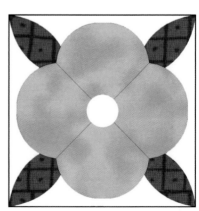

Molly's Rose Garden

3 Add the circle to the center of the flower to complete the block.

From The Kansas City Star, January 28, 1942

No. 676

9" block - pieced.

The leaves and center of this figure are appliqued on. The quilt is considered by its contributor, Miss Emma May Asbell, Jerico Springs, Mo., as especially attractive when set together with blue.

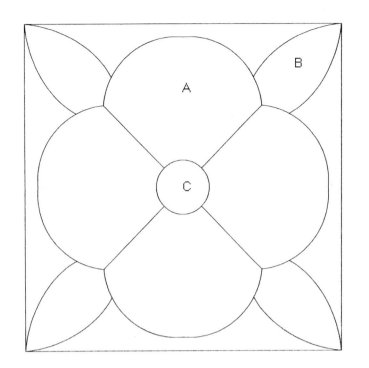

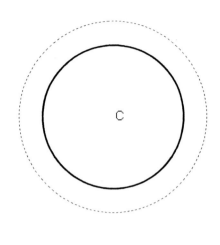

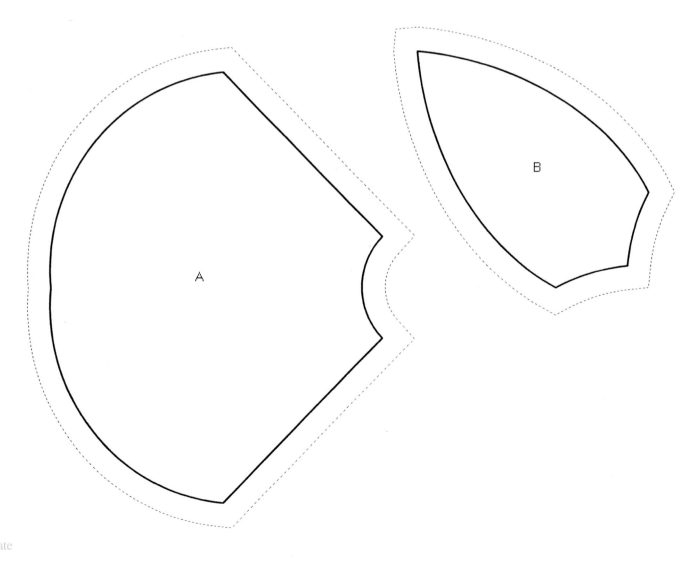

Molly's Rose Garden

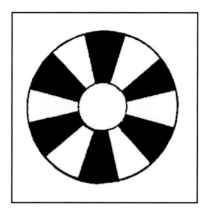

From The Kansas City Star,

June 4, 1952:

Number 908

Pieced and Applique - original size 11"

The design is from Mrs. Dessie Walters, route 3, Pawnee, Ok., daugther of a pioneer Oklahoma farmer. Develop your wagon wheels as you like them, in gay or somber tones, for truck or parade transport.

From The Kansas City Star:

June 20, 1955.

Old-Fashioned Wagon Wheels

No. 954

Pieced - original size 10 1/2"

A subscriber of many years to Weekly Star Farmer and an enthusiastic quilt piecer, Mrs. T. A. Best, Locust Grove, Ok., has offered this conception of an old-fashioned wagon wheel. She developed her block with alternate strips of 1-tone blue and blue and red print on a white background. The red hub of her wheel is appliqued with blue thread. Mrs. Best's choices are only suggested colors. The wedges may be alternate one tones of different colors or one tones alternating with prints that carry one or more of the 1-tone wedge colors.

A

B

A

B

Template

Appeared in The Star **May 11, 1960**

Rope and Anchor

Block Size: 9" finished

Fabric Needed

Brown

Blue print

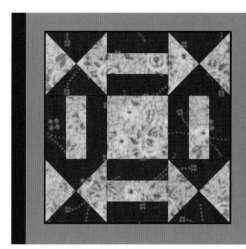

To Make the Block

1 Sew a blue triangle to a brown triangle. Make two and sew them together. You now have a quarter-square triangle unit. Make 4 – one for each corner of the block.

2 Sew the rectangles together as shown. Make 4.

3 Sew a quarter-square triangle unit to each end of a strip unit. Make two.

4 Sew a strip unit to either side of the blue square.

You can make this block using rotary cutting instructions or templates.

Cutting Instructions

From the brown fabric, cut

2 – 4 1/4" squares. Cut each square from corner to corner twice on the diagonal, or use template A.

8 – 1 1/2" x 3 1/2" rectangles or use template B

From the blue fabric, cut

2 – 4 1/4" squares. Cut each square from corner to corner twice on the diagonal, or use template A.

4 – 1 1/2" x 3 1/2" rectangles or use template B

1 – 3 1/2" square

Rope and Anchor

**From The Kansas City Star,
May 11, 1960**:
No. 1048.

Original size - 8 1/4"
This maritime theme, the Rope and Anchor, is most effective when developed in two colors. Like any marquetry skill is required in cutting the pieces and in putting them together to preserve the straight lines. The design is an offering of Amelia Lampton, Aguilar, Colo.

Our pattern for the week
also ran as Broken Dish in
August 21, 1937:
No. 516.

Original size - 9"
This may be in any plain color and white to suit the room in which it is to be used. The Broken Dish is also called Rope and Anchor design. It is sent by Mrs. A. L. Stimpson, Galt, Mo.

5 Sew the three rows together to complete the block.

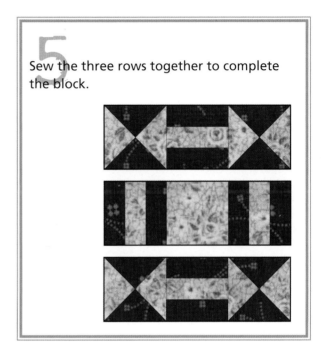

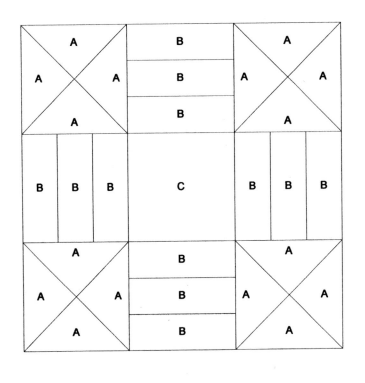

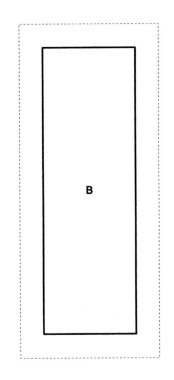

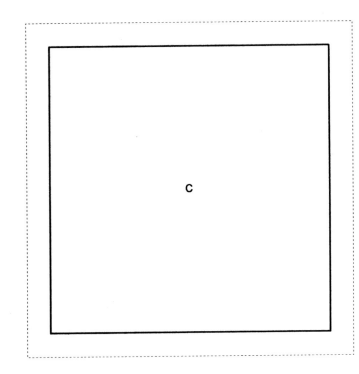

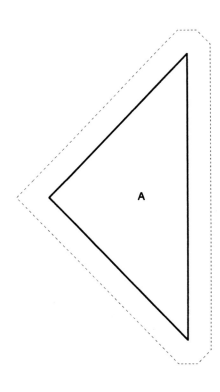

Template

Prickly Pear

Block Size: 14" finished

Fabric Needed

Black

Red

Tan

Cream

You can make this block using rotary cutting directions.

Cutting Instructions

From the black fabric, cut

8 – 2 1/2" squares (template A)

From the red fabric, cut

10 – 2 7/8" squares or 20 triangles using template B

2 – 4 7/8" squares or 4 triangles using template C

From the cream fabric, cut

2 – 4 7/8" squares or 4 triangles using template C

5 – 2 1/2" squares (template A)

From the tan fabric, cut

10 – 2 7/8" squares or 20 triangles using template B

To Make the Block

1 You will need to make half-square triangles. To make half-square triangles using rotary cut squares, draw a line from corner to corner on the diagonal of the lightest fabric. Sew 1/4" on each side of the line. Cut along the drawn line, using your rotary cutter. Open each unit and press toward the darkest fabric.

Make 20 half-square triangles using the tan fabric and the red fabric. If you are using the templates, sew the red B triangles to the tan B triangles.

2 Make 4 half-square triangles using the red fabric and the cream fabric. If you use the templates, sew together the red C triangles to the cream C triangles.

3 Sew all the units into rows as shown below.

Prickly Pear

4 Sew the rows together to complete the block.

From The Kansas City Star, October 3, 1931:

No. 190

Original size – 15 3/4"

"The prickly pear" is an old-time pattern which every quilter changed to suit herself. Today the pattern is an elaboration of the two patterns. The block is 15 inches or a little larger and is used with alternating blocks of plain material. Allow for seams.

History of the Block

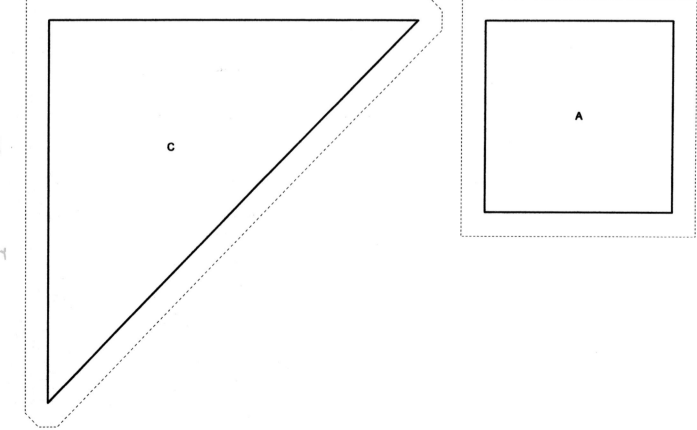

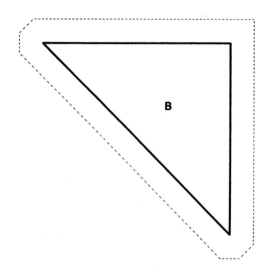

Prickly Pear

Template

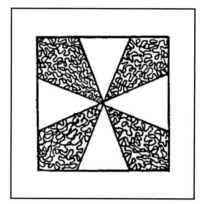

From The Kansas City Star,

October 30, 1957:

No. 1013

Original size – 6 1/2" block - pieced.

An imaginative conception of the square dance as it is done in Oklahoma is depicted by Emma W. Swicegood, Tulsa.

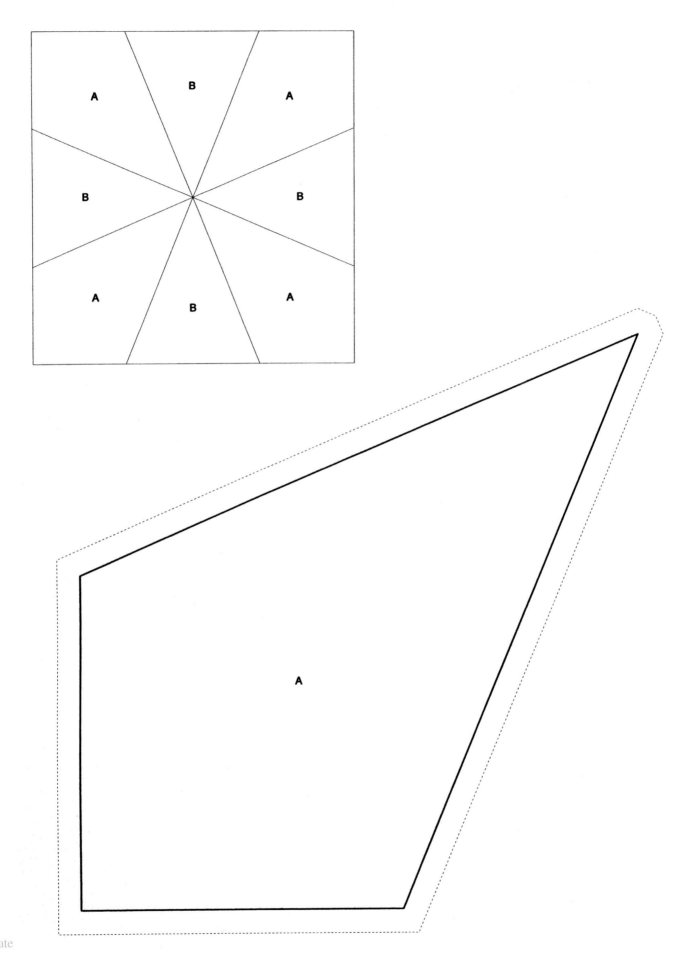

Template

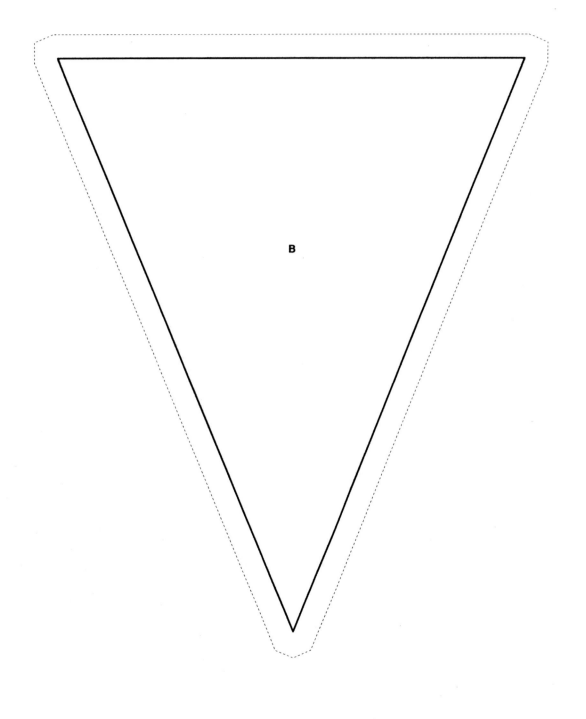

B

Template

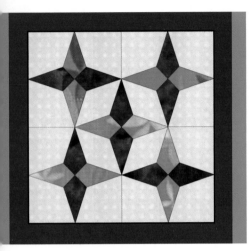

Pontiac Star

Block Size: 12" finished

Fabric Needed

Dark blue

Medium blue

Cream

We'll be using templates for this block.

Cutting Instructions

From the dark blue fabric, cut

10 pieces using template B

From the medium blue fabric, cut

10 pieces using template B

From the cream fabric, cut

12 pieces using template A

4 diamonds using template C

To Make the Block

1 Sew the medium blue and dark blue pieces together forming a star as shown. Make 5.

2 Inset the cream A pieces to three outer edges of four of the stars.

3 Inset the cream A pieces to three outer edges of four of the stars.

4 Inset the cream A pieces to three outer edges of four of the stars.

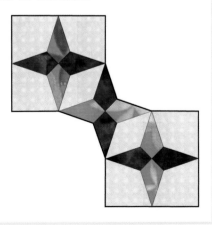

5 Add the upper right and lower left stars to complete the block.

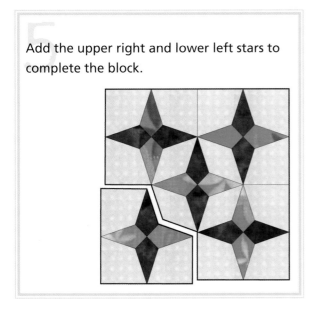

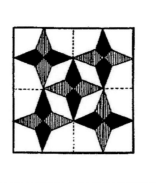

From The Kansas City Star,

February 21, 1931:

No. 158

Original size – 12"

A simple lesson in quilting is the piecing of this very pretty star pattern called "Pontiac Star" because of its arrowhead motif. The stars are placed in an interesting arrangement. To make a perfect pattern one should watch the position of these stars very carefully in putting the quilt together. The block is twelve inches square and is alternated with plain material the same size. Allow for seams.

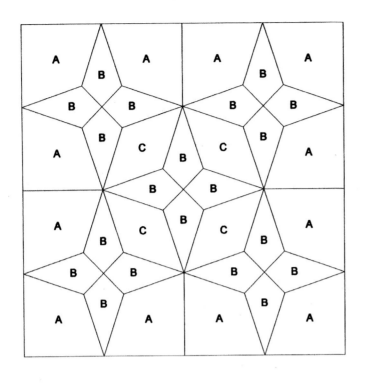

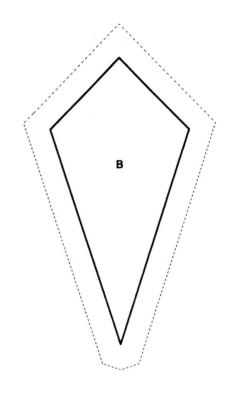

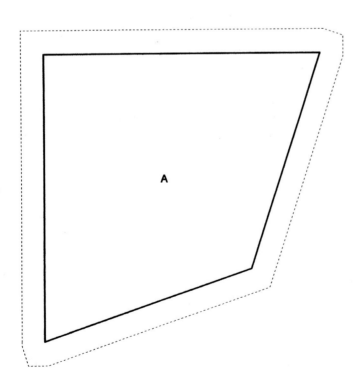

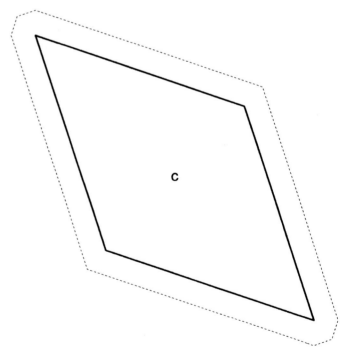

From The Kansas City Star,

October 17, 1928:

No. 5

Original size – 5 1/2"
This quilt gets its name from the appearance of the light blocks being cut out to add to the dark, while the dark blocks are trimmed to piece out the light blocks. This procedure is not exactly the case, however, as in reality the blocks must be larger to provide for a seam. Make a cardboard cutting pattern from the sketch given above. This pattern does not allow for seams, so draw on the cloth around the cardboard but cut a seam larger and then sew to the pencil line. Rob Peter and Pay Paul looks like a series of circles when set together, but the unit block is square, as shown in the small sketch at the left. Of course, half of the blocks are made with dark centers and half with light centers surrounded by the darker color. Blue and buff are suggested but any two harmonizing colors make up attractively in this charming old-fashioned design. Patterns of both the center block and parts of the circle are given in the cut in correct size.

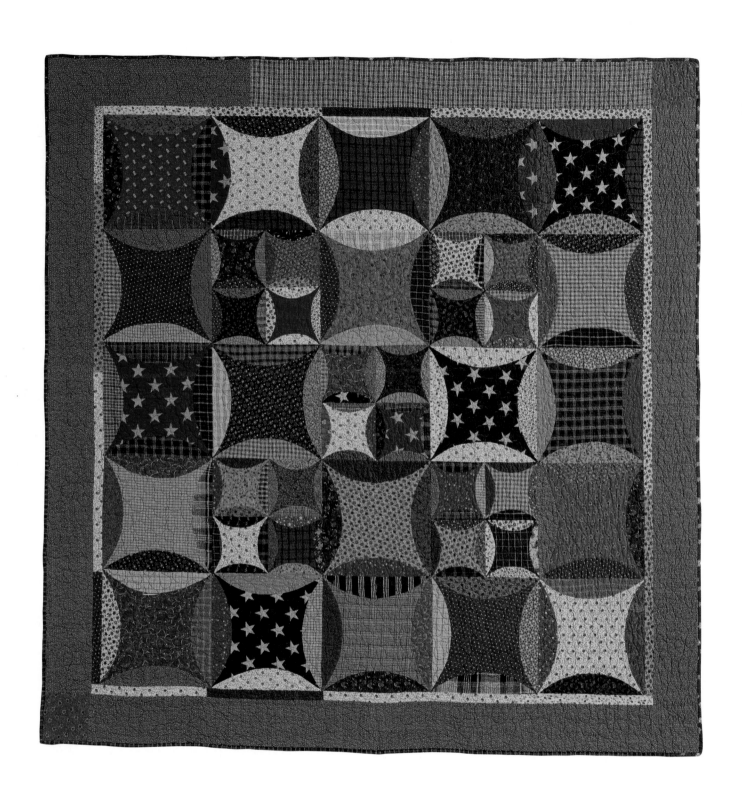

Peter, Paul and Aunt Mary designed by Lynda Hall, Apopka, FL.
Quilted by The Olde Green Cupboard Staff, Jacksonville, FL.

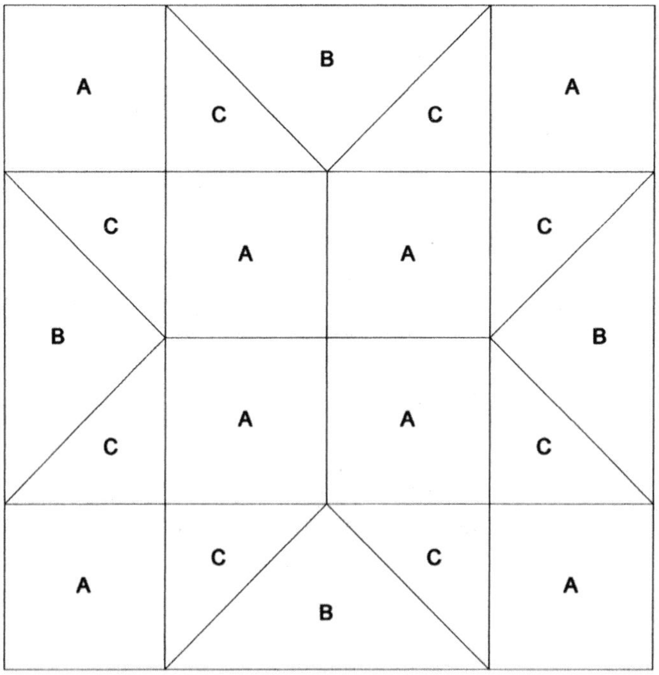

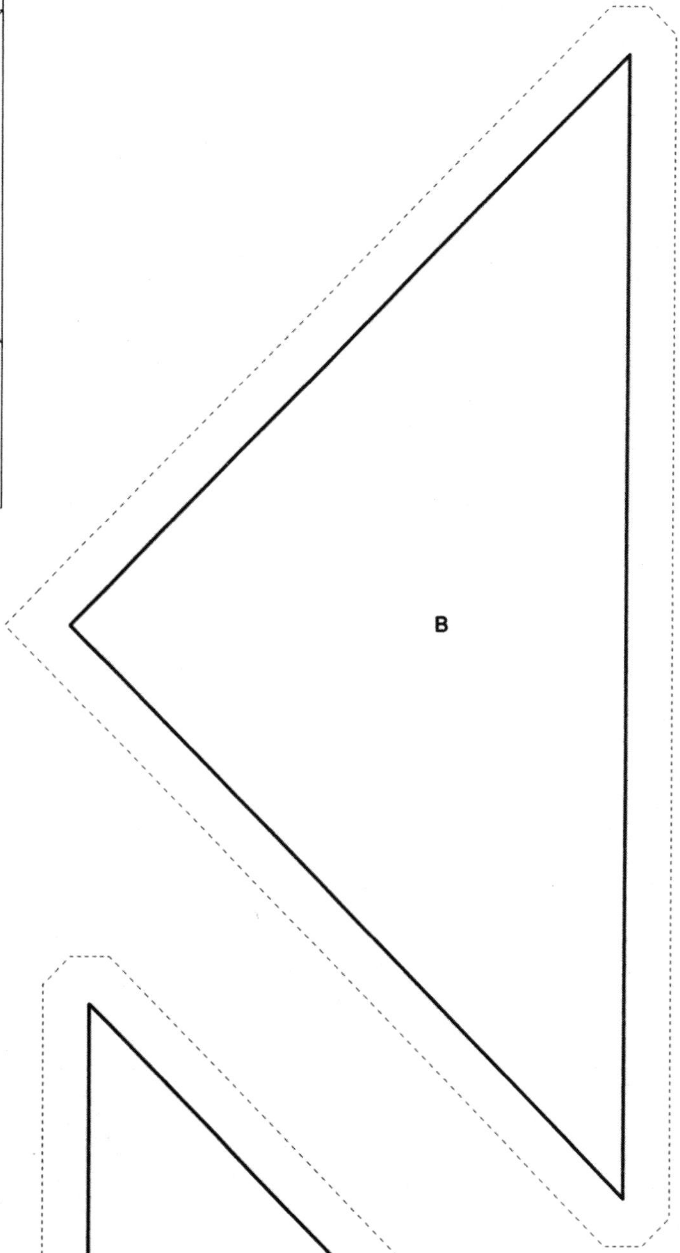

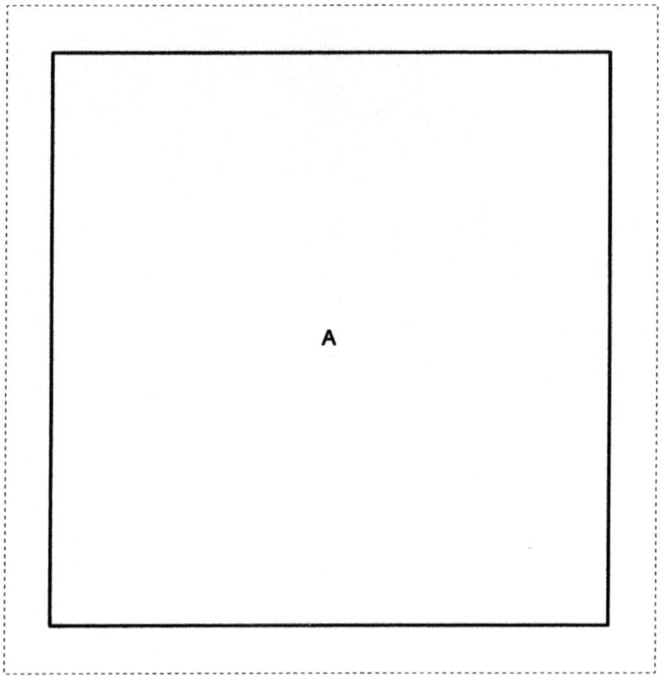

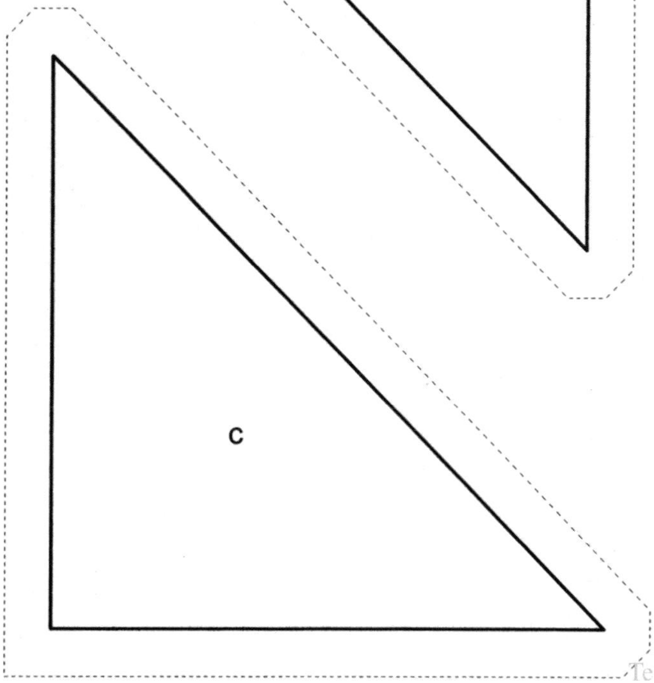

A B C

A C A C A

B C A A C B

C A A C

A C B C A

B

C

A

Winged Four Patch

Template

Victory Quilt

Block Size: 6" finished

Fabric Needed

Red

Tan

You can make this quilt block using rotary cutting instructions.

Cutting Instructions

From the red fabric, cut

2 - 3 7/8" squares or 4 triangles using template A.

From the tan fabric, cut

2 – 3 7/8" squares or 4 triangles using template A.

To Make the Block

1 Draw a line from corner to corner on the diagonal on the reverse side of the tan squares. Place a tan square atop a red square with right sides facing and sew 1/4" on either side of the line. Using your rotary cutter, cut on the line. Open each of the half-square triangle units and press toward the red fabric. If you cut your triangles using the template, sew the red and tan triangles together.

2 Sew the half-square triangles together as shown. Make two units like this.

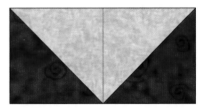

Victory Quilt

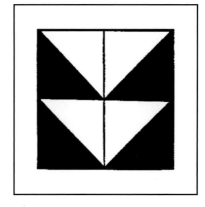

From The Kansas City Star,

April 8, 1942:

No. 682

Pieced - original size – 8"
This charming old pattern usu-
ally is made in white and gold
but is lovely in any combination
of colors. Allow for seams.

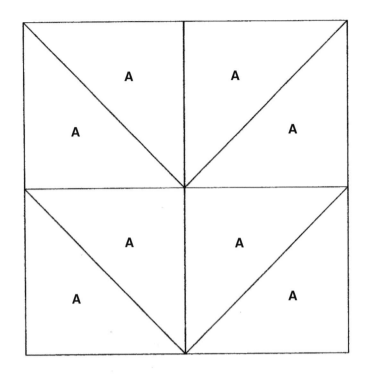

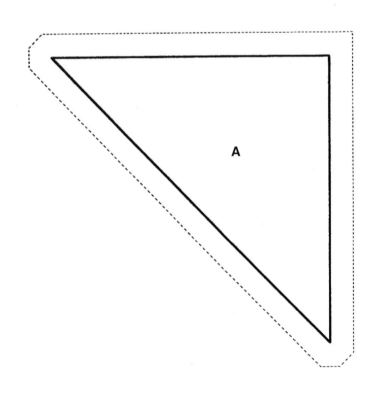

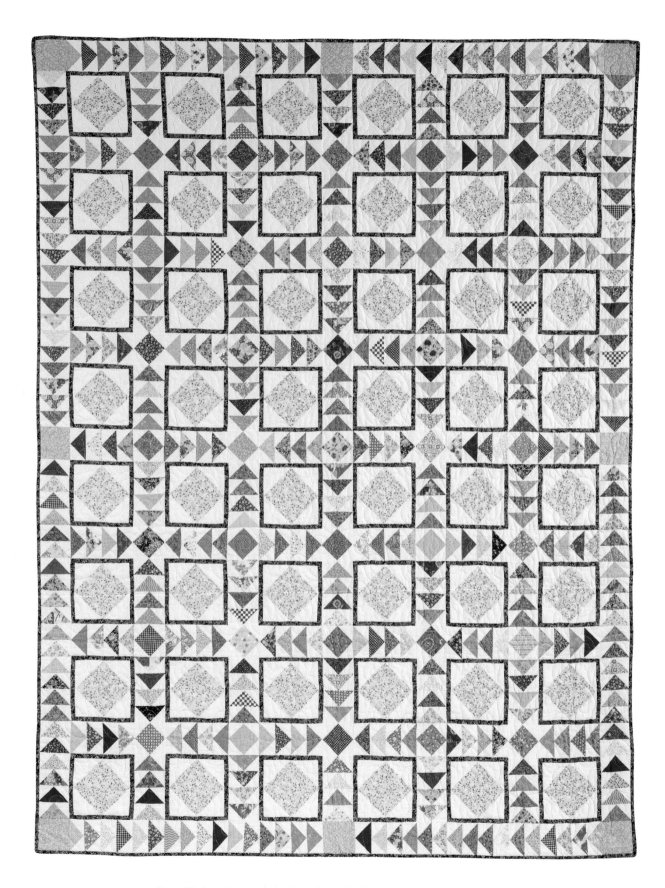

Just Flying Around designed by Sunisa Cote, Sammamish, WA.
Quilted by Deborah K. Burnett, Simpsonville, SC.

Road to Arkansas

Block Size: 12" finished

Fabric Needed

Light

Dark

Cutting Instructions

From the light fabric, cut

10 – 2 1/2" squares (template A)

2 – 4 7/8" squares (or cut 4 triangles using template B)

From the dark fabric, cut

10 – 2 1/2" squares (template A)

2 – 4 7/8" squares (or cut 4 triangles using template B)

To Make the Block

1

Draw a line from corner to corner on the diagonal on the reverse side of the light 4 7/8" squares. Place a light square atop a dark square with right sides facing and sew 1/4" on either side of the line. Using your rotary cutter, cut on the marked line. Open the half-square triangle units and press toward the dark fabric. You need 4 half-square triangles.

If you chose to cut the triangles using template B, sew the light and dark triangles together to make 4 half-square triangles.

2

Sew the light and dark squares together to make four-patch units. You will need to make 5 of them.

3

Sew the half-square triangles and the four-patch units together as shown to complete the block.

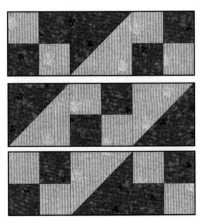

Road to Arkansas

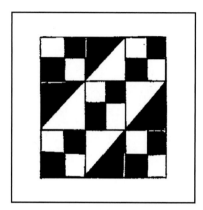

From The Kansas City Star,

June 6, 1956:

No. 984

Original size - 12" – pieced. Reminiscing about the trails over which she has walked and driven, stirred the fancy of Maxine Loosey, Old Joe, Ark., with the above result.

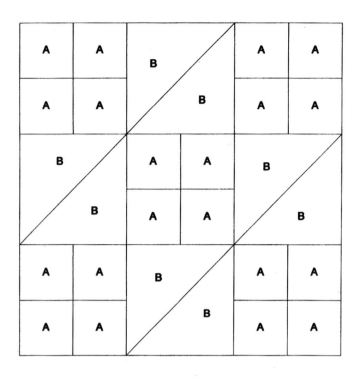

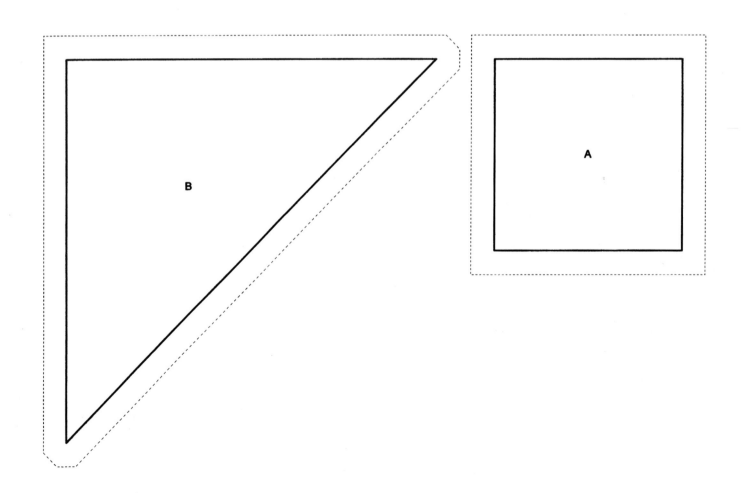

Appeared in The Star **September 22, 1934**

Whirling Pin Wheel

Block Size: 12" finished

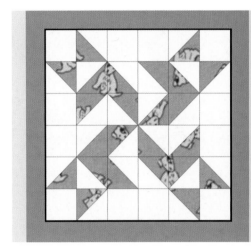

Fabric Needed

Medium blue

Light blue

To Make the Block

You will need to make half-square triangles. To make half-square triangles using rotary cut squares, draw a line from corner to corner on the diagonal of the lightest fabric. Sew 1/4" on each side of the line. Cut along the drawn line, using your rotary cutter. Open each unit and press toward the darkest fabric. If using templates, sew together a light blue B triangle and a medium blue B triangle. Make 24 half-square triangles using the light blue fabric and the medium blue fabric.

Sew the squares and half-square triangles into rows as shown below.

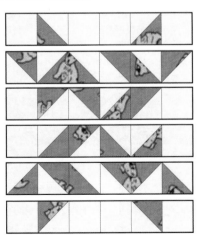

You can make this block using rotary cutting directions.

Cutting Instructions

From the medium blue fabric, cut

12 – 2 7/8" squares or 24 triangles using template B

From the light blue fabric, cut

12 – 2 7/8" squares or 24 triangles using template B

12 – 2 1/2" squares (template A)

Whirling Pin Wheel

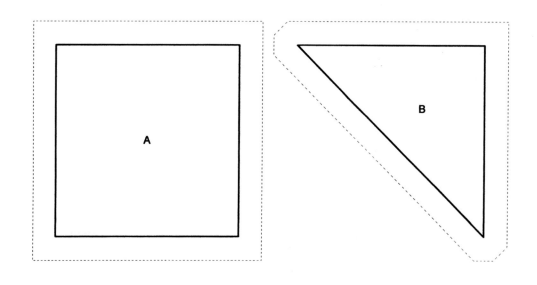

Appeared in The Star **May 10, 1930**

Merry-Go-Round

Block Size: 12" finished

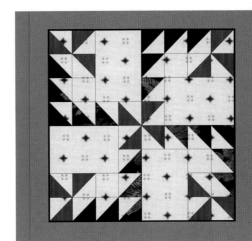

Fabric Needed

Black

Red

Cream shirting

Cutting Directions

From the black, cut:

10 – 2 3/8" squares or 20 triangles using template A

From red, cut:

8 – 2 3/8" squares or 16 triangles using template A

From the cream shirting, cut

18 – 2 3/8" squares or 36 triangles using template A

4 – 3 1/2" x 5" rectangles or use template B

4 – 2" squares or use template C

To Make the Block

1 You will need to make half-square triangles. To make half-square triangles, draw a line from corner to corner on the diagonal of the lightest fabric. Sew 1/4" on each side of the line. Cut along the drawn line, using your rotary cutter. Open each unit and press toward the darkest fabric. Make 16 half-square triangles using the cream shirting and the red fabric and 20 half-square triangles using the cream shirting and black fabric.

2 Sew one red/cream half-square triangle to one black/cream half-square triangle. Sew the unit to the cream rectangle. Make 4.

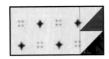

3 Sew two red/cream half-square triangles to a cream square then add a black/cream half-square triangle.

Merry-Go-Round

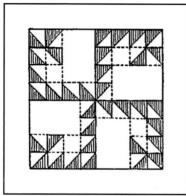

From The Kansas City Star,

May 10, 1930:

No. 96

Original size - 18"
This block is an admirable design for using odd scraps of bright wash goods, since each block may be a different color so long as the light and dark value remains about the same. The thing that makes so many old quilts disreputable looking is a few really dark blocks, navy blue or lead-colored percale irregularly spaced and showing up like great holes in an otherwise light colored patterns of pinks, yellow and pale blue. There must be a plan for the whole quilt when using scrapbag pieces. These cutting units may or may not be cut a seam larger than the sizes here given. "The Merry-Go-Round" as shows is really four blocks, all exactly alike.

4 Now sew one red/cream half-square triangles and three black/cream half-square triangles together as shown. Make 4.

5 Sew the units together to make one-fourth of the block. Make 4.

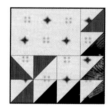

6 Sew the units together as shown below to complete the block.

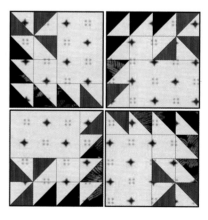

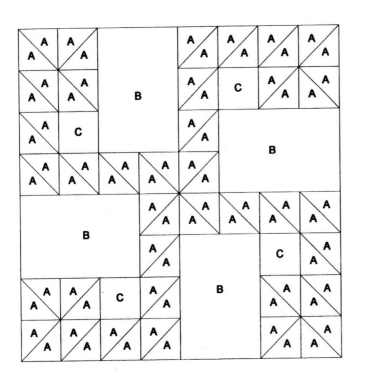

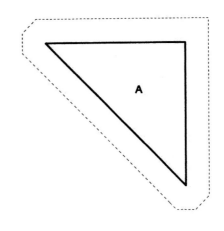

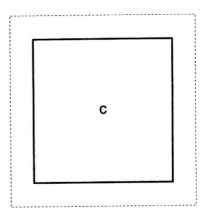

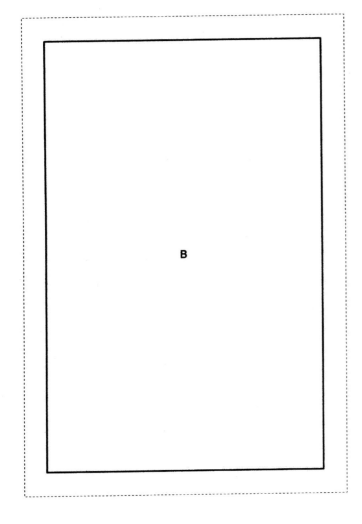

Merry-Go-Round

Template

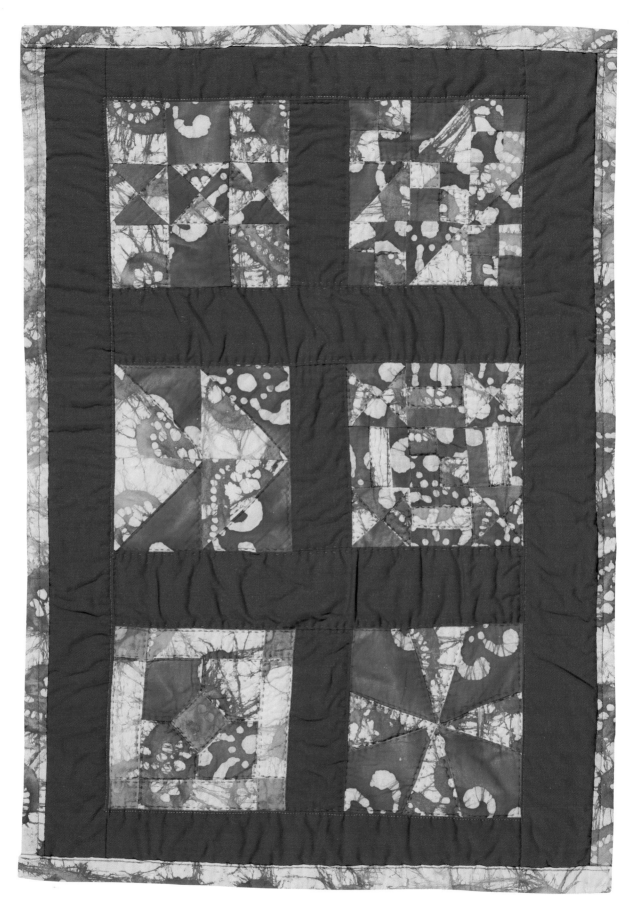

Little Jewel designed and quilted by Karen Davidson, Purdy, MO.

My Stars

Patterns from *The Kansas City Star* • Volume I

My Stars II

Patterns from The Kansas City Star • Volume II

My Stars III

Patterns from The Kansas City Star • Volume III

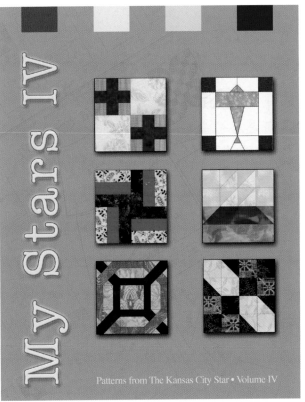

My Stars IV

Patterns from The Kansas City Star • Volume IV

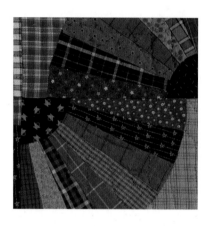